中英双语版

企鹅经典　名人大发现

克劳德·莫奈

［美］安·沃尔德伦（Ann Waldron）◎著　［美］斯蒂芬·马凯西（Stephen Marchesi）◎绘　高琼◎译

Who Was Claude Monet?

CNS　湖南科学技术出版社　小博集 BOOKY KIDS

·长沙·

著作权合同登记号：字18-2024-196

图书在版编目（CIP）数据

名人大发现. 克劳德·莫奈 : 汉英对照 /（美）安·沃尔德伦（Ann Waldron）著 ; 高琼译 ; （美）斯蒂芬·马凯西（Stephen Marchesi）绘. -- 长沙 : 湖南科学技术出版社，2025. 1. --（企鹅经典）. -- ISBN 978-7-5710-3269-2

Ⅰ. H319. 4

中国国家版本馆CIP数据核字第20249607HG号

上架建议：科普读物

QI'E JINGDIAN · MINGREN DA FAXIAN：ZHONG-YING SHUANGYU BAN KELAODE MONAI

企鹅经典 · 名人大发现：中英双语版　克劳德 · 莫奈

著　　者：［美］安 · 沃尔德伦（Ann Waldron）
绘　　者：［美］斯蒂芬 · 马凯西（Stephen Marchesi）
译　　者：高　琼
出 版 人：潘晓山
责任编辑：刘　竞
策划出品：李　炜　张苗苗　文赛峰
策划编辑：马　瑄
特约编辑：杜佳美
营销编辑：付　佳　杨　朔　周晓茜
装帧设计：利　锐
内文排版：金锋工作室
出　　版：湖南科学技术出版社
（湖南省长沙市芙蓉中路416号　邮编：410008）
网　　址：www.hnstp.com
印　　刷：三河市航远印刷有限公司
经　　销：新华书店
开　　本：875 mm × 1230 mm 1/32
字　　数：106千字
印　　张：5.125
版　　次：2025年1月第1版
印　　次：2025年1月第1次印刷
书　　号：ISBN 978-7-5710-3269-2
定　　价：22.00元

若有质量问题，请致电质量监督电话：010-59096394　　团购电话：010-59320018

目　录

谁是克劳德·莫奈？ / 001
第一章　一个热爱绘画的男孩 / 005
第二章　曲折坎坷的开始 / 018
第三章　艰难时期与顺利时期 / 042
第四章　一场新“沙龙展” / 054
第五章　最艰难的时期 / 062
第六章　吉维尼 / 070
第七章　花园和睡莲 / 090

克劳德·莫奈生平年表 / 102
世界大事记 / 103
莫奈画作馆藏一览表 / 104

Contents

Who Was Claude Monet? / 105

Chapter 1 A Boy Who Loved Drawing / 107

Chapter 2 A Rocky Start / 113

Chapter 3 Bad Times and Good Times / 125

Chapter 4 A New "Salon" / 131

Chapter 5 Hardest Times / 135

Chapter 6 Giverny / 140

Chapter 7 The Garden and the Water Lilies / 149

Timeline of Claude Monet's Life / 156

Timeline of the World / 157

Bibliography / 158

Where to Find Monet Paintings / 159

谁是克劳德·莫奈？

克劳德·莫奈给绘画创作注入了阳光。

他是第一批在户外创作的画家之一。户外作画对我们来说可能并不罕见，然而，1870 年以前，大多数画家的所有画作都是在画室里完成的。他们让模特打扮成希

腊诸神或历史英雄，创作时使用深色的绘画颜料，这样做可以使他们的画作看上去更“庄重严肃”。有些时候，他们可能会到户外去创作某个场景，不过最终的成品画总是在画室里完成的。

克劳德·莫奈和他的画家朋友们打破了这些惯例。即使在巴黎当艺术生时，他们也把画架、颜料和画笔拿到户外去画河堤、画树林。他们去海边，一画就是一整天。

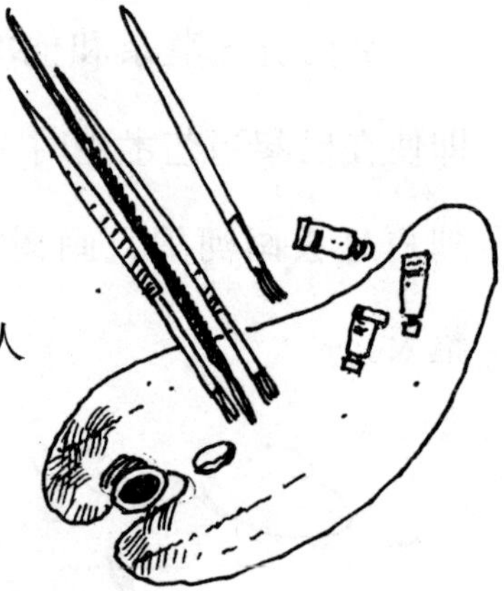

他们想表现阳光在一天中不同时间里让水、树木和船只呈现出的样子。假如他们创作的是人物画，画中的人便是衣着普通的普通人。他们用鲜艳明快的颜色快速创作。

数年来，莫奈几乎没有赚到钱。他有时候付不起房租，有时候家里供不起暖气，有时候填不饱肚子。即便境况如此窘迫，莫奈依然没有放弃绘画创作。

如今，莫奈是有史以来最著名的画家之一。他的画作售价高达数百万美元，在世界各地的博物馆里展览。令我们大家感到幸运的是，克劳德始终相信自己的艺术风格。

第一章

一个热爱绘画的男孩

画家克劳德·莫奈于1840年11月14日出生于法国巴黎。不过，在他五岁那年，他们举家搬到了勒阿弗尔，那是一个著名的港口城市。

小克劳德不喜欢上学。他就读的学校只在上午和下午各开课两个小时。尽管如此，他还是几乎无法忍受学校生活。待在学校里让他一直觉得就像待在“监狱”里一样。每当阳光灿烂的时候，他就想去户外，到田野中，或者到海边。终其一生，他都是一个不愿墨守成规的人。

克劳德的父亲是一个杂货商，专门向停靠在港口的大船的船长们出售物资。

克劳德喜欢去码头。他喜欢看人们从船上卸下货物，其中有南美的红木、西印度群岛的蔗糖、爪哇岛的咖啡

豆、印度的茶和波斯的枣子。他还喜欢听船上的人讲各种外语。

姑妈玛丽－让娜

克劳德十六岁的时候，他的母亲去世了。由于他姑妈玛丽－让娜没有生养孩子，所以她帮忙抚养克劳德。

克劳德身材高大挺拔，性格乐观开朗。他一直热爱绘画，一开始，他给自己想象中的动物画素描，也给自己的老师画漫画。

克劳德还报名参加过绘画班。老师教他的方法是当时人们教绘画的常规方法：学生们首先画石膏雕像的素描，数年后才可以学习画人物写生。等学生上绘画课的时间足够长之后，再让他们学习上色。

克劳德既不喜欢绘画老师也不喜欢上绘画课。他坚持自己的绘画，用铅笔或钢笔画勒阿弗尔人的速写。一个售卖美术用品的商店把他的画装裱起来展示在橱

窗里。就这样，克劳德卖出去许多幅画。

后来，这个商店老板把他介绍给当地的一位画家。这位画家名叫欧仁·布丹，他热衷于画风景油画——以大自然为对象的油画作品。布丹邀请克劳德白天和他一起绘画。克劳德一开始拒绝了他。因为布丹的风景小油

画售价比克劳德的漫画低得多。后来的一个夏日里，他让步了，买了一些油画颜料，跟随布丹一起去了乡下。

布丹是为数不多的在户外创作的画家之一。当克劳德看到他的新朋友把天空和田野画得如此真实时，他的眼睛为之一亮。

油　画

莫奈年轻的时候，社会上特别盛行反映历史场景或者神话传说的大型油画。一位画家可能得耗费数周、数月，甚至一年的时间才能完成这样的一幅油画。这类油画的每一处轮廓线条都非常清晰，不存在柔和或模糊的线条。它们的创作目标指向绝对完美的成品画。这就要求画作至少涂上三层颜料。

莫奈创作油画作品之前，画家们已经用了四百年油画颜料，当时的法国画家还在使用这种颜料。他们不得不自己研磨色料块，自己调制颜料。他们的绘画使用了很多大地色系的颜料，他们没有办法制作出优质的亮绿色颜料。

一直到19世纪中叶，专门用于油画创作的新颜料才出现。画家们有新上市的、更加鲜艳的颜色可以使用了。大约就在同一时间，油画颜料制造商想出办法把油画颜料装入带有螺纹盖的软

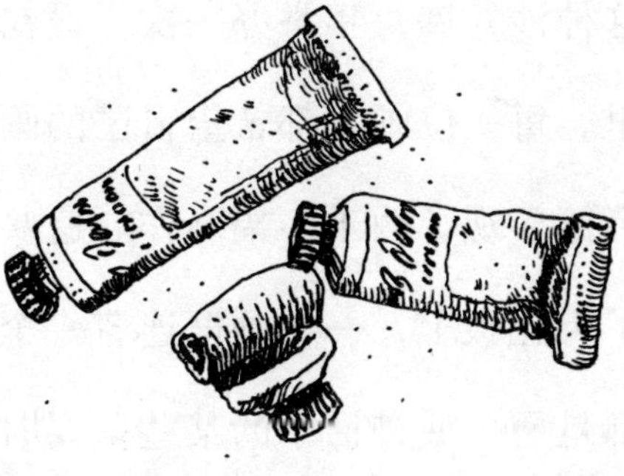

管中。现在，画家们可以把他们的颜料随身带到户外去了。

这件事对印象派画家而言，来得真及时！

从此，克劳德的生活发生了改变。

他想要去巴黎学习油画。而他父亲想让他从事杂货生意。不过，克劳德得到了姑妈的鼓励。她姑妈本人也是一位画家。1859 年，他离开勒阿弗尔前往巴黎。当时克劳德十八岁。他售卖漫画获得的收入足够支付他所需的费用。

巴黎是一座五光十色的城市，那里咖啡店、夜总会和博物馆林立。克劳德去参观了被称为沙龙展的著名美术展览。这种沙龙展每年举办一次，设在一个有玻璃屋顶的大厅里。每一位画家都希望自己的画作出现在沙龙展上。克劳德参观了两千多幅画作。这些画作从地板上一直挂到了天花板上，一个画框连着一个画框。所有画作展现的都是历史或神话中的某些重要时刻。克劳德对此类作品根本不感兴趣。他认为这类作品一看就让人感觉沉闷压抑。

他报名参加了瑞士学院的绘画班，课程是免费的。学生们只需要拿出一点钱用来支付使用模特的费用。之

后，他们想怎么画就怎么画。他们可以画素描，可以画油画，也可以画水彩画。他们可以画真人模特，也可以画静物。无论是清晨还是深夜，他们随时都可以去画室。对克劳德来说，这种生活简直像待在天堂一样幸福。

克劳德孜孜不倦地作画。这期间，他与一个年纪比自己大的同学交上了朋友。此人名叫卡米耶·毕沙罗。此后他们两人成了一辈子的朋友。

莫奈喜欢住在巴黎。不过，这段激情澎湃的时光于 1861 年结束了。

这是为什么呢?

因为克劳德不得不加入法国军队。

卡米耶 · 毕沙罗

第二章

曲折坎坷的开始

参军后，莫奈被派往北非的阿尔及利亚。他喜欢那里的热和光。他觉得睡在沙漠的帐篷里是一件很浪漫的事。

当时法国军队的服役期为七年。不过，两年之后莫奈得了伤寒病，请病假被送回了家。

约翰 · 巴托尔德 · 容金德

那年夏天，回到勒阿弗尔的莫奈继续在户外作画。这期间，他偶遇一位荷兰画家——约翰 · 巴托尔德 · 容金德——他跟布丹一样，在户外进行绘画创作。莫奈后来说，容金德和布丹两人都是他的老师。

祖阿夫轻步兵部队

莫奈于 1861 年加入祖阿夫轻步兵部队，这个部队的第一批士兵征召自阿尔及利亚祖阿夫地区。后来，像克劳德·莫奈这样的法国人也应征入伍了。

祖阿夫轻步兵部队助力法国征服阿尔及利亚，还在非洲领土以外的战争中为法国而战。他们在第一次世界大战中发挥了重要的作用。

祖阿夫士兵身穿华丽的制服，全红（夏装）或者全白（冬装）的长裤塞进黑皮靴里，黑皮靴的靴筒差不多到膝盖，靴子闪闪发亮。他们胸前系着宽腰带，上身穿着长外套，外套上垂着金线流苏。头上戴着一顶小帽子。

莫奈的姑妈觉得他的成品画作看上去像粗糙的草图。不过，克劳德在绘画创作上有多么勤奋努力，她都看在眼里。所以她给政府付了一笔钱让克劳德永久退伍。之后，她把他送到巴黎去了。他父亲承诺，假如他师从正统的绘画老师，就给他一笔资助。就这样，莫奈又参加了绘画班。

莫奈的新老师认为他是一位非常优秀的画家。然而，他希望克劳德把模特画得比实际的样子好看些。假如模特的两只脚太大，他认为克劳德应该把它们画小一些。

莫奈对此表示不认同。完全不认同！他认为眼睛看到的是怎样的，笔下画的就应该是怎样的。他也不喜欢在一个拥挤而吵闹的画室里作画。不过，在这样的绘画课堂上，也会发生美妙的事情。其中三位同学——皮埃尔－奥古斯特·雷诺阿、阿尔弗雷德·西斯莱和弗雷德里克·巴齐耶——成了克劳德的挚友。数年来，他们几个一起创作。巴齐耶原本是医科生，只要他能继续医学院的学业，他的父母就会为他支付绘画课的学费。雷诺阿十三岁的时候就开始创作瓷画。和莫奈一样，为了能来巴黎，他攒了足够的钱。西斯莱很幸运，他们都这样说。他本来是英国人。他父亲恰巧在巴黎经商，无条件地资助儿子学习绘画。

莫奈的朋友们

莫奈1862年在夏尔·格莱尔画室学习期间，与弗雷德里克·巴齐耶、皮埃尔－奥古斯特·雷诺阿和阿尔弗雷德·西斯莱成了好朋友。

弗雷德里克·巴齐耶

巴齐耶于1841年生于法国蒙彼利埃市的一个富裕家庭。他经常与莫奈在户外从事绘画创作，不过他的绘画作品更为传统。1870年普法战争爆发时，巴齐耶加入了祖阿夫轻步兵部队。就在同一年，他在战争中被杀了。

雷诺阿于1841年出生于法国利摩日市的一个工人家庭，其父为裁缝。雷诺阿爱好绘画，创作出了许多栩栩如生的人物肖像画，还画了很多反映社交生活场景的画作。他的职业生涯漫长而富有成就，最终于1919年逝世。

西斯莱于1839年出生于法国巴黎市，他的父亲母亲都是英国人。莫奈和雷诺阿经常创作反映城市生活或者社交场景的画作，西斯莱的绘画作品的核心关注点却是自然景色。他于1899年逝世。

皮埃尔－奥古斯特·雷诺阿

巴齐耶和西斯莱尽管不如莫奈或雷诺阿那么出名，但是他们俩的画作被美国和欧洲的许多著名博物馆收藏。

莫奈跟他的这几个新朋友谈及户外创作的事情。起初，其他人并不感兴趣。雷诺阿说服莫奈和他一起去卢浮宫临摹画作。

然而，即便莫奈在博物馆内支起了画架，但创作出来的却是他透过窗户看到的景色！

摄 影

1859 年，照片首次出现在巴黎的沙龙展上（莫奈第一次参观沙龙展的一年之前）。

摄影这种新的艺术形式影响了当时的年轻画家们。照片反映日常生活——比如，穿着现代服装的普通人。照片捕捉到一个个瞬间。这正是莫奈想做的事情。此外，因为摄影提供了一切事物的真实画面，因此，莫奈与他的朋友们觉得如今的画家更加自由，绘画创作可以不那么逼真了。他们可以从主观视角来探索光线与颜色的效果。

摄影师们经常到户外去摄影，他们扛着庞大笨拙的照相机到莫奈喜欢作画的那些地方去。他们经常把摄影设备放置在画家的画架旁边。

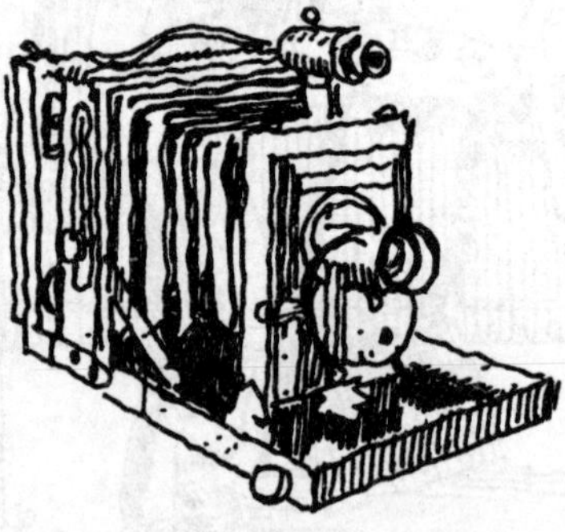

最后，莫奈终于说服他的新朋友们去参观一片大森林附近的一个美丽小镇。于是他们收拾好画架、颜料盒、画布和画笔，出发了。朋友们在户外画速写，然后回到画室去完成画作。然而，莫奈本人的所有创作活动都在户外进行。他已经开始尝试捕捉阳光以及阳光和阴影落在树木和草地上的效果。

1864 年，绘画学校关闭。此后莫奈再也没有上过绘画课。他回到了勒阿弗尔的家。他的家人受够了他。因为他除了在学生时代售卖过自己创作的漫画以外，再也没有卖出过一幅画作。他应该开始用正统的技法绘画了！

这些话莫奈听进去了吗？当然没有。他出发到海边去，在户外作画。1865 年，他把两幅画作寄到沙龙展……两幅画作都被接收了！

他激动万分。当时的报纸对他的画作大加赞赏。这两幅画都卖了一大笔钱。

带着对这次成功的兴奋，他开始创作一幅新的巨作。他拟用的画布长二十英尺[①]，宽十五英尺。对如此巨大的一块画布，著名的老派画家们经常会用来创作历史场景。不过，莫奈头脑中的想法不同。他想要画十二个人，他们身穿日常服饰在野炊。他邀请朋友们来为画作摆造型。在如此巨大的画布上进行户外创作太不容易了。因此，很遗憾，莫奈不得不打破自己定下的规则，把画布拿进室内创作。他特别希望这幅新画能走进沙龙展，不过他没能及时完成创作。

相反，他为自己美丽的新女友卡米尔快速画了一幅真人大小的肖像画。她皮肤白皙，头发乌黑。画中的她身穿一条有条纹的绿色裙子，打着一把遮阳伞。同样因为时间关系，这幅画他也是在画室里创作完成的。《绿衣

① 英美制长度单位。1 英尺 ≈ 0.305 米。

女子》于1866年被沙龙展接收，获得了成功。

莫奈的父亲和姑妈对此感到十分高兴吗？不！他们勃然大怒。因为他们发现莫奈和卡米尔已经同居了，但两人还没有结婚。为此他父亲又一次中断了对他的资助。

那一年克劳德二十五岁，卡米尔十九岁。他们没有钱——事实上他们还欠着债。于是他们只能离开巴黎，去到一个小镇上租房居住。在那里，莫奈开始创作另一幅大型画作，虽然不如野炊画那么巨大，但依然是一幅大型画作。其规格为八英尺长、七英尺宽，展现的是花草树木间的四位女子。四位女子的造型全都由卡米尔一人负责。莫奈发誓，从此以后自己的每一幅画作都在户外完成。他在花园里挖了一条沟渠。这样的话，当他想在画布的顶部作画时，他就可以把画布放下来。

一天，另一位画家经过，问他为什么不开始作画。

“太阳还没有出来呢。”莫奈回答。

他的朋友建议他至少可以先画背景。不过莫奈解释说，画作的每一个部分——即便是背景——都必须在阳光下创作。这是他绘画创作的核心要点。

1867年举办的沙龙展拒绝接收他的大型新作《花园里的女人》。这幅画作太与众不同了。评委们认为，照射在连衣裙和遮阳伞上的阳光以及树木投下的影子看上去陌生、怪异。

莫奈陷入绝望，几乎要丧失理智。尽管如此，他还是坚持作画。因为他没钱买画布，所以有时候用刮刀刮下先前画作的颜料，这样他就可以在旧画布上创作新画了。

巴齐耶对莫奈的窘境深感难过，便花钱把他的《花园里的女人》买了下来。他还答应每个月给莫奈寄些钱来。不过有很多次他都忘记寄钱了。莫奈非常绝望，因为卡米尔快要生小孩了，可是有些时候他们的钱都不够买食物。

莫奈陷入了困境。他带着卡米尔去了巴黎。在那里，他卖出去两幅画，转而把钱给了卡米尔，这样她才有赖以生存的经济条件。

随后，莫奈独自一人回到勒阿弗尔。这次他决定跟父亲母亲撒个谎，说他跟卡米尔已经分手了。

回到勒阿弗尔后，他发了疯似的努力工作，把赚到的每一分钱都寄给卡米尔。他创作了二十幅画——包括人物画、风景画和海景画。最重要的是，他希望孩子出生时自己有充足的经济条件与卡米尔待在一起。不过，

1867 年 8 月 8 日，小让出生的那一天，他的父亲并不在他身边。

最终，莫奈的姑妈十分同情他，帮他支付了前往巴黎的火车票。那时候，他、卡米尔和小宝贝一家三口租住在一个小房间里。那年冬天天气特别冷，家里有时候供不起暖气，也没有足够的食物。

那段时间，莫奈无论走到哪里，厄运似乎像影子一样跟着他。他的画作卖不出去，因此他、卡米尔和小宝贝只能搬到乡下一个更便宜的住处。然而，等到他也无

法支付房租的时候，房东太太把他们一家三口赶了出去，却把他的衣服、画布、颜料和画笔扣留下来了。

此时此刻，除了还剩家人之外，莫奈已经一无所有了。

第三章

艰难时期与顺利时期

对莫奈来说，他很难想象自己的境况还会变得更糟糕。幸运的是，他的运气终于改变了……至少有了些许好转。勒阿弗尔的一位富翁想要买画——购买莫奈的画作。他想要购买几幅肖像画。就这样，莫奈以最快的速度完成了画作。这位富翁还购买了他的两幅海景画。

莫奈拿着这笔钱，在勒阿弗尔附近的一个海滨小镇为自己的小家庭租了一间小屋。他继续在户外创作，尝试在画作中融入光线和阴影的元素。他对光线进行了研究，让画作中的光线看起来生动逼真。在画阴影的过程中，他开始使用不同颜色的颜料代替黑色颜料。他不再在调色板上调制混色。相反，他直接在画布上画纯色。他如果需要绿色，就在黄色边上轻轻来上一笔蓝色。在看画作的时候，他的眼睛会把蓝色和黄色融合在一起，看到的就会是绿色。他曾经这样说：“到户外创作的时候，尽量忘掉你面前有什么东西，树木、房子、田野，诸如此类的景物。脑子里只想着，这里是一个小小的蓝色正方形，那里是一个粉色的长方形，这里又是一道黄色的条纹，然后把你眼里看到的颜色和形状不折不扣地画出来。”

那年夏天，莫奈经常和他的老朋友皮埃尔－奥古斯特·雷诺阿待在一起。两位画家在户外肩并肩进行绘画创作。那个时候莫奈依然很穷。雷诺阿也很穷，不过，他是跟父母住在一起的。雷诺阿有时候会给莫奈的家人捎来一些面包，以免他们饿肚子。

他们朋友二人可能经济窘迫，可能吃不饱。但是，他们热爱自己正在从事的绘画创作事业。他们两个人同时画了这样一幅作品：塞纳河上的一家快乐、热闹的露天餐馆。阳光照耀着人们和桨船，在水面上投下美丽的影子。这两幅餐厅画后来都成了名画。

然而，1870 年举办的沙龙展再一次拒绝了莫奈的画作。他最好的几个朋友——巴齐耶、雷诺阿、西斯莱和

毕沙罗——无一例外，都有画作被沙龙展接收。

那是一段艰难的时光。不过那一年也发生了一件好

事。卡米尔的父母说，假如她跟莫奈结婚，他们就会原谅她，甚至会帮忙抚养小让。就这样，克劳德和卡米尔结婚了。婚礼在巴黎举行，莫奈的家人一个也没有出席。

之后，新郎、新娘和小让前往勒阿弗尔附近的一个海边度假村。布丹和他的妻子在那里跟他们会合。莫奈在海边给妻子卡米尔作画。这些年来，他为她创作了许多幅画作——有站在山坡上的，有站在花田里的，有打着遮阳伞的，有站在花园里的。而小让经常在她身边。

那年 7 月，法国与普鲁士交战（当时的普鲁士是今天德国的一部分）。因为莫奈需要养家，所以他跑到了英国以逃避兵役。

日本版画

有一天，莫奈买了一些包装好的食品杂货，他发现包裹用的纸张上画着日本版画。

跟其他许多印象派画家一样，莫奈对这些木刻版画非常着迷。印象派画家对这些用色明快、风格平面化以及构图经常偏离中心的作品甚是赞赏。多年以来，莫奈收集了许多日本著名画家的版画。这些画作至今挂在他位于吉维尼的家中。日本版画激发了他的灵感，他在吉维尼的池塘上建造了一座日本桥。

跟之前在法国一样，他在伦敦也疯狂地进行绘画创作。随后，好运第二次降临在他头上。一位年纪比他大的法国画家把他介绍给了一位重要的画商。此人名叫保罗·迪朗－鲁埃尔。他不但在巴黎拥有一个画廊，在伦敦也拥有一个画廊。迪朗－鲁埃尔见识了莫奈的才华，于是购买了好几幅他的画作，而且出价很高。

保罗·迪朗－鲁埃尔

普法战争结束后，莫奈并没有立即返回法国，而是带着妻儿举家来到荷兰。他们在阿姆斯特丹附近安顿下来。在那里，莫奈画了运河、风车和郁金香。

1871 年，他们返回法国，在塞纳河上的一个小镇租了一座房子。莫奈一直喜欢临水而居。最重要的是，他酷爱以水为主题进行绘画创作。那一年他完成了差不多五十幅作品。

终于，莫奈真正开始赚钱了。他的家人有足够的食物了。莫奈买了一只驳船，并把驳船改造成了一个水上画室，这样他就可以置身河流中央来创作了。

此时的法国处于和平时期，时局稳定。迪朗－鲁埃尔回到巴黎，又从莫奈那里买了更多画作。这期间，莫奈画了河流、田野、卡米尔和让待在户外的画。那是一段快乐的时光。

第四章

一场新“沙龙展”

一年又一年，莫奈的画作总是被沙龙展拒之门外。大多数情况下，他的三个朋友——雷诺阿、毕沙罗和西斯莱——也会被拒绝。即便评论家认为他们的画作看上去“粗糙”，给人一种“未完成”的感觉，但他们全都认为自己的画作看起来清新生动。

莫奈认为，假如他们想赚钱，就必须举办他们自己的画展。

因此，在 1874 年，他们就这么干了。

他们的画展比沙龙展早两周举办，三十位画家参加了他们的画展。

每天只有一百人左右来参观他们的画作，而成千上万的人拥向沙龙展。

参观者中有人拿他们的画展开玩笑。画展上卖出去的画作不多。对画布上星星点点的明亮颜料，人们不解其意。他们说这些画家一定有一把装了颜料的枪，并用它朝画布开了火。他们拿莫奈的画作开了最多的玩笑。一位评论家写道："莫奈先生……似乎已经对美宣战了。"

莫奈有一幅画作描绘的是冉冉升起的红日下的两只小船。这幅画作需要在展览目录中拟个标题。莫奈决定将其命名为《日出・印象》。他为什么选择这样一个名字呢？因为莫奈和他的朋友们经常说，绘画时捕捉场景的第一印象有多么重要。

人们拿这个标题开玩笑。很快，所有在画展中展出作品的画家都被称为“印象派画家”。这个称呼原本是一种侮辱。不过，莫奈和其他印象派画家对此欣然接受，认为自己的确是印象派画家。

这些印象派画家在接下来的几年里继续举办画展。在 1875 年举办的一次画展上，为了阻止人们用手杖和雨伞破坏画布，警察不得不出来维持秩序。画展上只卖出了几幅画，而且价格极低。

莫奈又一次向朋友借钱。1876 年秋天，卡米尔生病了，境况看起来确实很悲惨。

莫奈再一次被拯救了，这一次拯救他的是一位富有的艺术品收藏家。这位名叫埃内斯特的收藏家与他的妻子艾丽斯买下了许多印象派画作。他们是巴黎一家百货

艾丽斯和埃内斯特

公司的股东，在离巴黎不远的地方有一处宽敞、漂亮的住宅。埃内斯特邀请莫奈住在他家，为家里的一个房间画几幅画。

1876 年的整个夏天，莫奈都待在埃内斯特家作画，有段时间卡米尔和让也过来跟他待在一起。他们享用着美味的食物，享受着仆人的伺候，还有彼此令人愉悦的

陪伴。这段时间对体瘦抱病的卡米尔来说一定是一段美妙的休养时光。

一回到巴黎，莫奈便醉心于创作以火车站为主题的画作。他画人群，画巨大的黑色火车头冒出的蒸汽，画透过车站玻璃屋顶看到的天空。一位站长非常乐意为莫奈提供帮助。假如莫奈因为绘画创作需要白烟，站长一定会吩咐火车司机喷出白烟。

然而，在接下来的一次印象派画展上，参观者也不喜欢以火车站为创作主题的画作。其中一位参观者甚至要求退票。莫奈从绘画创作中赚到的钱很少。为了支付购买颜料的账单，他不得不把自己的十六幅画卖给了艺术用品经销商。最糟糕的是，卡米尔身体越来越虚弱。而且她也快要生另一个孩子了。

第五章

最艰难的时期

莫奈的第二个孩子是一个小男孩，取名为米歇尔，他出生于 1878 年春天。卡米尔的健康状况每况愈下。埃内斯特失去了所有的钱，因此他和妻子艾丽斯还有他们的六个孩子都搬来跟莫奈一家同住。大家一起住在一座

大房子里，房子里有通往塞纳河的陡峭台阶。

艾丽斯管理家务，还负责照顾卡米尔和小宝贝米歇尔。她还给别人上钢琴课获得收入。埃内斯特从来不支付他的那份家庭开支，账单堆积如山。

那是一个漫长而艰难的冬天。寒冷的天气都打破了历史记录。11 月 29 日开始下第一场雪，整个 12 月份都在下雪。积雪达到好几英尺深。火车经常停驶。道路经常被大雪阻断。塞纳河结冰的时候，孩子们开开心心地到河对岸的小镇去。然而，大人们却忧心忡忡、苦不堪言。莫奈继续从事户外绘画创作。为了尽可能保持身体的温度，他有时候身上穿着三件外套，并携带一个热水瓶。

困境中，一个邻居拯救了他们。他出钱购买了莫奈的部分画作，这样莫奈家里的每个人都不用挨饿了。

那一年，莫奈给印象派沙龙展寄去了二十九幅画作。玛丽·卡萨特，一位居住在巴黎的美国画家，她以三百美元的价格购买了其中一幅画作。不过，很多人还是觉得莫奈的绘画风格看上去很怪异。一位艺术评论家说他一定是在一个下午就完成了这二十九幅画作。

除了缺钱带来的问题以外，卡米尔还患了癌症，生命垂危。莫奈拼命想办法支付卡米尔的治疗费和医药费，为了尽可能多地筹集现金，他把所有能典当的东西都典当了。

平生第一次，莫奈无法进行绘画创作了。

1879 年 9 月 5 日，卡米尔在极度痛苦中离世了。

莫奈决定在卡米尔临终前为她画最后一幅画，尽管这个决定听起来让人觉得奇怪。他惊讶地发现，尽管内心悲伤，自己还是注意到了光线照在爱妻静止不动的脸庞上的样子。画作中，她的样子不像一位宁静的天使，而像一位去世的女士。他跟一个朋友坦诚地说，他是艺术的奴隶。对他来说，没有什么比艺术更重要了。

艾丽斯和她的六个孩子依然跟莫奈以及他的两个儿子住在一起。第二年冬天仍然寒冷。塞纳河再次彻底冻结。八个孩子全都生病了。

那年冬天，莫奈又开始创作，他产出了许多以塞纳河为主题的画作。他孜孜不倦地研究着光线照在冰上、雪上的样子。冰雪融化时，大块大块的冰顺着塞纳河漂流而去。莫奈采用暗灰色和深紫色两种颜色把这个景象画了下来。他把这些画作拿出去销售时，每个人都说这些作品的“未完成感”比他平时的作品有过之而无不及。

他也到勒阿弗尔附近的一个海边小镇去画海景画。一天，天上下起了大雨。一场暴风雨即将来临。莫奈决定努力把这个景象画下来。他把画架架在悬崖之上，俯瞰大海，用绳子把画架固定下来。海浪拍击着他脚下的悬崖，他仍在作画。海浪越来越高，莫奈一直不停地画。

这时，一个巨浪袭来，把他从高高的悬崖上卷到水中。莫奈差点被卷进了大海。他紧紧抓住系在画架上的绳子才幸免于难，得以生还。最后，是路过的一艘船上的两个渔夫把他救了上来。

这次历险之后不久，莫奈把大家庭迁到了一个离巴黎更近的住处。那里有一所适合小让上学读书的好学校。如今，艾丽斯和她的六个孩子成了这个家庭的永久成员。艾丽斯觉得莫奈的两个儿子需要她照顾。

一家人在新房子里没住多久。莫奈说他在那里无法创作，因为光线不好。然而，就在 1882 年，他赚的钱比以往任何时候都多。当塞纳河洪水泛滥，把房子的一楼给淹没的时候，莫奈不再在这个地方待下去了。是时候找一处光线充足的适宜住所，让自己能够安顿下来创作了。

他访遍了塞纳河沿岸的村庄，最后终于找到了一座对他来说近乎完美的房子。房子位于一个叫吉维尼的小镇。他在那里一待就是四十三年，余生都在那里度过。

第六章

吉维尼

莫奈第一次见到吉维尼是在 4 月的一天。苹果树上开满了花，田野里的野花生机勃勃、闪闪发光。

当时的莫奈正坐在火车上。但看到眼前的美丽景色，他下了火车。只见主干道的右侧有一间大农舍在招租。农舍非常漂亮，粉色的墙壁，石板屋顶，灰色的百叶窗。房子的两侧各有一个低矮的谷仓，谷仓的地面是泥做的。

房子附带面积达两英亩[①]的土地，包括一个苹果园和一个围墙围起来的花园。一条小路通向铁路，铁轨的另一边流淌着一条小河。

---

① 英美制面积单位。1 英亩≈4046.86 平方米。

对画家来说，这就是一个理想的所在。在这里，莫奈可以看到沿河的柳树和各种各样的植物，还有草场边上的一排排高大的白杨树。“在这里我可以创作出传世杰作。”莫奈说。

一开始，他只是把房子租了下来（后来，他干脆买了下来）。一家人带着所有的家具和莫奈的桨船搬到了这里。现在他拥有四只船——一只当水上画室的桨船，两只划艇和一只小型帆船。他把画室船停泊在一个叫荨麻岛的地方。从家里走到荨麻岛很容易。

莫奈把其中一个泥地谷仓改造成一个画室。后来，他又建造了一个面积大得多的画室，画室开着天窗。他还搞了一个菜园。除草和浇水的活计由孩子们负责。他把花园四周的篱笆拆除了。这些篱笆看起来太齐整、太井然有序了。他也开始创作以大型花园为主题的画作了

（他最喜爱的花是鸢尾花）。他在人行道上方的金属拱门上种植了攀缘玫瑰，在花坛里种满了各种各样的草木和鲜花。他想保证自己的花园从早春到深秋一直都有鲜花盛开。

吉维尼的花园成了他生命中除绘画创作之外最重要的东西。花园也是一件艺术品。

莫奈是个作息规律的人。他每天日出时起床，吃些面包和香肠，然后用独轮手推车装着他的调色板、颜料和画架出发到户外去创作。他像当地农民一样，头戴贝雷帽，脚穿木制鞋。到了中午，他回家吃午饭。午饭一直是上午十一点半准时开始。午饭后，他会待在画室里喝上一杯咖啡，有时也喝一杯白兰地。随后，如果光线还充足，他便返回室外去创作。

假如莫奈对自己的画作感到满意，全家人都很开心。如果一幅画作完成之后没有达到自己的期望，他就把它扔掉。莫奈的脾气不好。有一次，他在画室船上创作，对画作的视觉效果非常不满意，气得把画布扔进了河里，随即把颜料和画笔也扔了下去。他发誓以后再也不作画了。

当然，第二天他改变了主意。很不巧，那天刚好是周日。没有一个艺术用品商店开门营业。莫奈给巴黎的一位绘画颜料经销商发去了一封电报。经销商打开商店，把莫奈需要的所有东西经由开往吉维尼的最近一个班次的火车寄送了过来。

很多事情都可能让莫奈心里烦躁不安。哪顿饭不合口味了，或者花园里哪根树枝掉落下来，都会令他勃然大怒。

尽管有这样糟糕的时刻，但日子比以往任何时候都要好得多。莫奈把注意力更多地投向孩子们——除了自己的儿子让和米歇尔，还有艾丽斯的孩子们。学校放假期间，八个孩子和艾丽斯全都跟着莫奈一起去乡下。他创作的时候，孩子们找了很多自娱自乐的法子。布朗什画画，米歇尔钓鱼，苏珊娜看书，艾丽斯缝补衣服，年纪较小的几个男孩子喜欢抓青蛙。夏天的时候，他们依次从船舱顶上跳入水中，离开画室船游泳去了。而当冬天来临时，他们则在结冰的河上滑冰。

莫奈当时四十多岁的年纪，高大英俊，留着大胡子。艾丽斯美丽、聪慧、待人和善。她理解莫奈，欣赏他的画作。1892 年，艾丽斯与莫奈结婚了。日子幸福地继续下去。

时至此时，大众的审美眼光在发生变化。人们开始欣赏印象派画作。莫奈赚到的钱更多了。他在吉维尼的家中雇了一名厨师和一名助理厨师。他最喜欢的菜肴之一为酒酿红豆。他还喜欢鹅肝和一种叫松露的优质蘑菇。

许多客人前来参观他在吉维尼的家。除了拥有一个人口众多的大家庭，莫奈还与许多朋友、画家和作家保持联系。他和艾丽斯也喜欢到巴黎去看望朋友。他们喜欢去听音乐会、看歌剧表演或摔跤比赛。

在艺术创作上，莫奈开始画系列作品。每个系列绘画展示的都是同一个景物或同一个场景，不同的只是光线。

这些系列绘画的第一个系列中有一幅画描绘的是一排排沿河而立的白杨树。针对白杨树这一个景物，莫奈清晨画一幅，然后大约在中午再画一幅，在傍晚又画一幅。他在多云的阴天画白杨树，在灿烂的阳光下画白杨树。他把一年四季——春天、夏天、秋天和冬天——的白杨树全都画了一遍。

一天，他听说自己最喜爱的那些白杨树有一部分要被砍下来当木材卖掉，便花钱让这些白杨树多保留几个月以便自己能把画作完成。

莫奈也画田野里的干草堆。这些干草堆有十五到

二十英尺高。就像画白杨树一样，他在一年中的不同时间段、不同的光线下一次又一次地画干草堆。他会推着一辆装满画布的独轮手推车来到田野。有时候，艾丽斯的某个女儿会推着另一辆独轮手推车，车上装着更多画

布跟着他一起去。

莫奈一开始在一张画布上作画。随着时间一分一秒地流逝，光线也在不断发生变化，这时他会把这张画布放在一边，开始在另一张画布上作画。第二天，他会返回到第一张画布上继续画。每天的同一时间，他在同一张画布上作画。让光线保持不变，这一点对他来说十分重要。

莫奈还创作了另一个著名的系列绘画——鲁昂市的一个大教堂。为了创作这些作品，他在教堂对面租了一个小房间，把画架立在窗户边。又一次，为了捕捉画作

的不同效果，他在云雾缭绕的日子绘画，在阳光明媚的日子绘画，在不同季节、一天中的不同时段绘画。结果，这个系列绘画非常受喜欢，大教堂画作卖了一大笔钱。而且，这些画作在全世界各地的画展中展出。

现在，莫奈出名了。

他的花园也出名了。陌生人前往吉维尼观赏他花园里的那些神奇的花。世界各地的画家前往吉维尼，希望向莫奈学习。（莫奈对他们说："好好看看大自然吧。"）曾经有一段时间，莫奈位于吉维尼的住所附近租住着四十多位美国画家。

吉维尼镇上开咖啡馆的女士学会了做美国游客喜欢的食物，比如烘豆。她甚至为他们准备了感恩节晚餐。有些美国人非常喜欢吉维尼，最后在那里买了房子。

艾丽斯和克劳德的孩子们逐渐长大成人了。让·莫奈在瑞士被培养成了一位化学家，随后他前往鲁昂市为他叔叔工作。让与艾丽斯的女儿布朗什恋爱了，之后结了婚。他们当时住在鲁昂市，不过他们每到周末都会回

咖 啡 馆

吉维尼。

米歇尔・莫奈与艾丽斯的儿子让 – 皮埃尔年纪相仿。

他们是继兄弟，但他们也成了非常亲密的朋友。他们两个都对花卉和植物感兴趣。让－皮埃尔甚至和一个家族

朋友写了一本关于该地区植物的书。

米歇尔和让－皮埃尔对自行车和发动机也很着迷。让－皮埃尔设计了一种带马达的双人自行车。米歇尔制造了一辆看起来像早期汽车的汽油动力汽车。

米歇尔从未外出工作过。他喜欢住在吉维尼的农场

里。莫奈喜欢让米歇尔待在自己身边。据说这对父子之间的交流从来不多。他们只是早上彼此简单地打个招呼，说声“早上好，莫奈”，上床睡觉前说声“再见，莫奈”。

第七章

花园和睡莲

莫奈花在花园上的时间和金钱越来越多。他给白垩土施肥。他买来珍稀植物。他为玫瑰搭建了更多棚架。他买了更多地当菜园，这样一来他就可以把花园里所有的花圃都用来种花了。他曾一度雇了六个园丁帮他干活。不过莫奈一直是负责人。

随着收入不断增多，莫奈有能力在家对面买些地了。流经那里的河水形成了一个

小池塘，池塘里长着慈姑和睡莲。莫奈在池塘里添加了更多不同种类的睡莲。几年之后，他又买了更多土地，以便扩大他的池塘。他不得不挖沟从河里引水来灌溉他的池塘。最终池塘比原来大了三倍。

1892年，他开始画睡莲。这可能是他最后，也最著名的绘画系列。他不仅画睡莲，也画睡莲在水中的倒影。

令人遗憾的是，艾丽斯患上了一种叫白血病的血液疾病。她的医生没有办法挽救她。她于 1911 年去世。

没有艾丽斯的日子，莫奈感到孤独、凄凉。他已经七十岁了。他经常感到头晕目眩、虚弱无力。最糟糕的是，他的视力正在衰退。他患上了白内障，虹膜上好像覆盖着一层厚厚的膜。白内障降低了他的眼睛对颜色的感知能力。

随之而来的是他的大儿子让·莫奈的离世。当时的让年仅四十七岁。之后让的妻子布朗什回到吉维尼来帮忙照顾她的继父。

因为悲痛和对自己眼睛的担心，莫奈一段时间内没有进行绘画创作。

当莫奈终于重新拿起画笔时，他开始创作更多的睡

莲画。他不再天一亮就开始创作，而是等到大约中午，睡莲开花的时候才开始画。1909 年，四十八幅睡莲画在巴黎的一个画展上展出。人们喜欢这些画作，说这些画作跟世界上的其他任何画作都不同。

乔治 · 克列孟梭

之后，他开始创作睡莲的巨幅壁画。这些画作比莫奈以前的任何作品都要大得多。他想把这些壁画永久陈列在一个巨大的圆形房间里。

1918 年第一次世界大战结束的时候，法国总理乔治 · 克列孟梭来到吉维尼。他是莫奈的朋友，请莫奈把睡莲画送给法国。莫奈同意捐出十二幅大型油画，条件是要把这些画作陈列在一个圆形房间里，参观者可以站在房间中央，周围被睡莲环绕着。

法国政府没有专门建造一座建筑。然而，卢浮宫博物馆附近有一座空房子。这座房子被称为橘园，因为它

曾经是法国皇室种植橘子树的地方。睡莲油画可以挂在一楼的两个椭圆形房间里。政府同意，那里不展出其他任何作品。

莫奈说，绘画是他生命中唯一能给他带来快乐的事情。然而，现在由于视力每况愈下，莫奈经常对自己的画作不满意。假如他不喜欢哪幅画，他总是想把它扔掉。他会把画布剪成碎片，尽管有时候米歇尔和布朗什会把画布碎片保存起来。

最后，他几乎双目失明的时候，家人们说服莫奈给他的眼睛做外科手术。经过两次手术，换上新的眼镜后，他的视力康复到可以绘画了。然而，此后他经常抱怨自己对颜色的感知能力差。

截至 1918 年，他已经完成了三十幅大型油画，但他拒绝出售其中任何一幅。他年近八十了。然而，他每天都要前往长着睡莲的池塘。两个园丁沿路帮他抬着画架和画布，为他的创作安排好一切。

他病得很重。莫奈一生都是老烟枪，后来得了肺癌。然而，直到 1926 年 12 月 5 日他去世的那一天，莫奈还在创作睡莲画。直到生命的最后一刻，他还在为他的花园做着新的规划。他很兴奋，因为已经有一些新的日本睡莲球茎到货了，他迫不及待要把它们种下去。

今天，人们蜂拥到博物馆参观莫奈的画作。他的巨幅睡莲画依然在橘园里展览。而更小的睡莲画在全世界的博物馆里展出。

米歇尔·莫奈去世时享年八十八岁。他没有孩子，因此他把父亲的许多美丽画作留给了巴黎的一家博物馆。其中一幅作品画的是日出时的小船，印象派因此作品而得名。

过去，莫奈常常吃不饱饭。可他的作品现在出售的价格之高一定会让他大吃一惊的。他在 1904 年创作的一幅睡莲画在 2007 年以三千六百八十万美元的价格售出。莫奈希望自己的作品能卖出去。但是，钱对他来说从来都不是最重要的。

当他的睡莲壁画第一次在橘园博物馆展出时，一位评论家惊叹于莫奈对水中花的神奇描绘，惊叹于他捕捉“稍纵即逝的瞬间”的惊人才华。

这个评论真实、准确地总结了莫奈毕生致力的事业——把大自然中稍纵即逝的瞬间画下来。

如今的吉维尼

克劳德·莫奈去世之后，他儿子米歇尔继承了那所房子。不过，他本人并未居住在那里。是他大哥让的妻子布朗什在料理房子和花园，一直到她 1947 年去世。

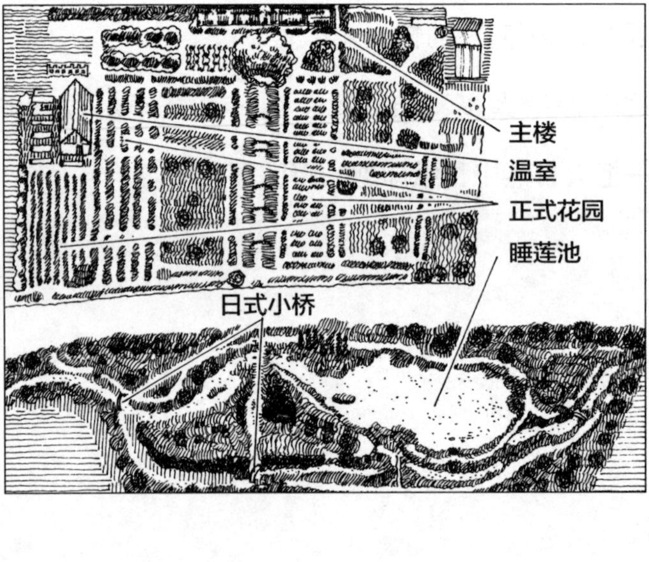

1966年米歇尔去世之后，好几个美国基金会帮忙筹钱，让房子和花园重现昔日的辉煌。如今，那所房子每年的4月到10月对公众开放。每年吸引着数以万计的参观者前往参观。

克劳德·莫奈生平年表

1840 年 — 克劳德·莫奈出生。

1858 年 — 莫奈遇见画家尤金·布丹。

1859 年 — 莫奈迁居巴黎并加入瑞士学院。

1861 年 — 莫奈加入祖阿夫轻步兵部队。

1862 年 — 莫奈遇见巴齐耶、雷诺阿和西斯莱。

1865 年 — 莫奈遇见卡米尔·东西厄。

1867 年 — 长子让出生。

1874 年 — 莫奈在第一次印象派画展中展出《日出·印象》。

1878 年 — 次子米歇尔出生。

1879 年 — 卡米尔去世。

1883 年 — 莫奈迁居吉维尼的家。

1892 年 — 莫奈与艾丽斯·贺西德结婚。

— 莫奈开始创作睡莲画。

1911 年 — 艾丽斯去世。

1914 年 — 让去世。

1926 年 — 莫奈去世。

1927 年 — 橘园博物馆展出《睡莲》系列画。

世界大事记

1840 年 — 世界上第一枚邮票“黑便士”发行。

1848 年 — 加利福尼亚淘金潮开始。

1853 年 — 文森特 · 梵高出生。

1860 年 — 弗洛伦丝 · 南丁格尔在英国创建了第一所正规的护士学校。

1865 年 — 美国宪法第十三条修正案废除了美国的奴隶制。

1870 年 — 普法战争爆发。

1876 年 — 马克 · 吐温的作品《汤姆 · 索亚历险记》出版。

— 亚历山大 · 格雷厄姆 · 贝尔发明了电话。

1886 年 — 自由女神像在纽约港落成。

1888 年 — 第一台柯达盒式照相机发售。

1889 年 — 埃菲尔铁塔在法国巴黎竣工。

1898 年 — 玛丽 · 居里发现了镭。

1901 年 — 华特 · 迪士尼出生。

1913 年 —《纽约世界报》首次出现填字游戏。

1914 年 — 第一次世界大战爆发。

1927 年 — 第一部有声电影《爵士歌手》首次上映。

莫奈画作馆藏一览表

你已经对克劳德·莫奈的生平有了颇为全面的了解，他的画作也值得你去参观。美国的很多博物馆至少收藏有一幅莫奈的画作。以下为永久收藏莫奈画作的大型博物馆：

美术博物馆——波士顿市，马萨诸塞州

芝加哥艺术学院——芝加哥市，伊利诺伊州

盖蒂博物馆——洛杉矶市，加利福尼亚州

大都会艺术博物馆——纽约市，纽约州

费城艺术博物馆——费城市，宾夕法尼亚州

国家美术馆——华盛顿特区

欢迎参观！

Who Was Claude Monet?

Claude Monet brought sunshine into painting.

He was one of the first artists to work outdoors. That may not sound unusual to us. But before 1870, most artists did all their painting in studios. They used models dressed up as Greek gods or heroes from history. They painted with dark colors so their pictures would look more "serious." They might have sometimes gone outside to draw a scene, but they always came back inside to paint the finished picture.

Claude Monet and his artist friends broke the rules. Even as art students in Paris, they took their easels and paints and brushes outdoors to paint riverbanks or woods. They made trips to the seashore and painted all day long.

They wanted to show the way sunlight made water and trees and boats look at different times during the day. If they painted people, they painted ordinary people in ordinary clothes. They used bright colors and painted quickly.

For years, Monet earned hardly any money. Sometimes he could not pay the rent; sometimes his family had no heat; sometimes they went hungry. Still, Monet would not give up.

Today, he is one of the most famous artists ever. Paintings by Monet sell for millions of dollars and hang in museums all over the world. We are all lucky that Claude never stopped believing in his art.

Chapter 1

A Boy Who Loved Drawing

The artist Claude Monet was born in Paris, France, on November 14, 1840. But when he was five, his family moved to Le Havre, a great seaport.

As a boy Claude hated school. His school was open only two hours in the morning and two hours in the afternoon. Still, he could barely stand it. School always made him feel like he was in “a prison.” When the sun was shining, he wanted to be outdoors, in the fields, or by the sea. Throughout his life he was a person who never wanted to stick by the rules.

Claude’s father was a grocer. He sold supplies to the captains of the tall ships in the harbor.

Claude loved to go down to the docks. He liked to watch the men unload cargo from ships. There was mahogany from South America, sugar from the West Indies, coffee beans from Java, tea from India, and dates from Persia. He liked to hear the men speaking foreign languages.

Claude's mother died when he was sixteen. His Aunt Marie-Jeanne had no children of her own so she helped to raise him.

He was a tall, cheerful boy. He always liked to draw. He began drawing pictures of imaginary animals and funny pictures of his teachers.

Claude also took drawing classes. His teacher taught the way everybody taught art then. Students first drew pictures of statues. After years of this, the students were allowed to draw living people. If they took classes long enough, the students would learn to paint.

Claude did not like the teacher or the class. He kept on with his own drawing, using a pencil or pen and ink to turn out quick sketches of people in Le Havre. A store that sold art supplies framed his drawings and put them in the window. Claude sold many of his pictures.

The store owner introduced him to a local painter. His name was Eugène Boudin. He liked to paint landscapes—pictures of nature. Boudin invited Claude to spend the day painting with him. Claude said no at first. Boudin's little pictures sold for far less money than Claude's cartoons. Then one summer day, he gave in and bought some oil paints. Then he set out with Boudin for the country.

Boudin was one of a handful of artists who painted outdoors. When Claude watched his new friend painting the sky and the fields exactly as they were, his eyes opened.

Claude's life changed.

He wanted to go to Paris to study painting. His father wanted him to go into the grocery business. But his aunt encouraged Claude. She, too, was a painter. In 1859, he left Le Havre for Paris. Claude was eighteen years old. The

Oil Paints

When Monet was young, large paintings of historical scenes or myths were very popular. It might take an artist weeks, months, or even a year to complete a painting. Artists used sharp outlines for everything; nothing was soft or blurred. They worked toward an absolutely perfect finish. This required at least three coats of paint.

Until just before Monet began painting, French artists were still using the same kinds of oil paints that artists had used for four hundred years. They had to grind their own pigments and mix their own paints. They used many earth-toned colors. There was no way to make good, bright, green paint.

By the mid-nineteenth century, new dyes for paints came along. Artists had new and brighter colors to use. About the same time, manufacturers figured out how to put oil paints in tubes with screw tops. Now artists could take their paints outdoors.

Just in time for the Impressionists!

money from his funny pictures was more than enough to support him.

Paris was a dazzling city with cafés, nightclubs, and museums. Claude went to see the great art show known as the Salon. It was held every year in a giant glass-roofed hall. Every artist wanted his paintings to be in the Salon. Claude saw more than two thousand pictures. They hung from floor to ceiling with their frames touching. All the paintings were the type that showed famous moments in history or myths. This type of art didn't interest Claude at all. He thought it looked depressing.

He enrolled in classes at the Académie Suisse, which was free. Students contributed a little money to pay for a model and worked on whatever they wanted to. They could draw or paint with oils or watercolors. They could paint a live model or they could work on a still life. They could come any time from early in the morning until late at night. For Claude it was like being in heaven.

Claude worked on his drawing. He made friends with an older student named Camille Pissarro. The two remained friends all their lives.

Monet loved living in Paris. But in 1861, this exciting time came to an end.

Why?

Claude Monet had to join the French army.

Chapter 2

A Rocky Start

Monet was sent to Algeria in northern Africa. He loved the heat and the light. He thought it was romantic to sleep in a tent in the desert.

Men were supposed to serve in the French army for seven years. But after two years, Monet caught typhoid fever and was sent home on sick leave.

That summer, in Le Havre, Monet continued to paint outdoors. He met a Dutch artist—Johan Barthold Jongkind who, like Boudin, painted outdoors. Jongkind and Boudin were his schoolmasters, Monet said later.

Monet's aunt thought that his finished paintings looked like rough sketches. But she saw how hard Claude worked.

Zouaves

The Zouaves was the military unit that Monet joined in 1861. The first regiments were made of men from the Zouave region of Algeria. Later on, Frenchmen like Claude Monet were enlisted as well.

The Zouaves helped France conquer Algeria and fought for France in wars outside Africa. They played an important role in World War I.

Zouaves wore dashing uniforms with full red or white trousers tucked into shiny black boots that came up almost to the knee. They wore a wide sash across their chest and a long coat with a gold braid. A small cap topped off the outfit.

So she paid the government to let Claude out of the army for good. Then she packed him off to Paris. His father promised him an allowance if he studied with a proper art teacher. So Monet tried more art classes.

Monet's new teacher thought that he was a very good artist. However, he wanted Claude to make the models better looking than they really were. If their feet were too big, he thought Claude should make them smaller.

Monet did not agree. Not at all! He thought you should paint what you saw. Nor did he like painting inside a crowded, noisy studio. But something wonderful came out of these classes. Three of the students—Pierre-Auguste Renoir, Alfred Sisley, and Frédéric Bazille—became close friends of Claude's. For years, they all worked together. Bazille was a medical student. His parents paid for his art classes as long as he kept up with medical school. Renoir had started work as a china painter when he was only thirteen. Like Monet, he had saved enough money to come to Paris. Sisley was

Monet's Friends

Monet became close friends with Frédéric Bazille, Pierre-Auguste Renoir, and Alfred Sisley while studying at Charles Gleyre's art studio in 1862.

Bazille was born in Montpelier, France, in 1841 to a wealthy family. He often painted outdoors with Monet, but his paintings were more traditional. When the Franco-Prussian war broke out in 1870, Bazille joined the Zouave army. He was killed in action that same year.

Renoir was born in Limoges, France, in 1841. He was the son of a working-class tailor. Renoir loved painting, and created many lively portraits and scenes of social life. He had a long and successful career. He died in 1919.

Sisley was born in Paris, France, in 1839 to English parents. While Monet and Renoir often painted urban life or social scenes, the natural landscape was the central focus of Sisley's artwork. He died in 1899.

Although not as famous as either Monet or Renoir, Bazille and Sisley have paintings in many famous museums in the United States and Europe.

the lucky one, they all said. He was English. His father was a businessman in Paris and paid for his son's art studies without conditions.

Monet told his new friends about painting outdoors. At first the others weren't interested. Renoir persuaded Monet to go with him to copy pictures at the Louvre Museum.

But instead Monet set up his easel inside the museum and painted what he saw outside the window!

Finally Monet convinced his new friends to visit a pretty little town near a huge forest. They packed up their easels, paint boxes, canvases, and brushes and headed out. His friends made sketches outdoors and then finished their paintings later at a studio. Monet, however, did all his work outdoors. Already he was trying to capture sunshine and the way light and shadows fell on trees and grass.

In 1864, the art school closed. Monet never took another art class. He went home to Le Havre. His family was fed up. He hadn't sold a thing since the funny pictures he did as a

Photography

Photographs were shown in the Paris Salon for the first time in 1859. (This was a year before Monet first visited the Salon.)

The new art of photography influenced young painters of the day. Photographs showed everyday life— ordinary people in modern clothes. They captured a moment in time. This is what Monet wanted to do. Also, because photography provided a realistic picture of anything, artists like Monet and his friends felt that painters were now free to be less real. They could be subjective and explore the effects of light and color.

Photographers often worked outdoors, carrying their huge cameras to the same places where Monot liked to paint. Often they set up their equipment beside the easels of artists.

schoolboy. He should start painting the proper way!

Did Monet listen? Of course not. He went off to the seacoast and painted pictures outdoors. He sent two to the Salon in 1865 . . . and both were accepted!

He was thrilled. Newspapers praised his work. Claude sold both paintings for a nice sum of money.

Happy with this success, he began a new huge picture. The canvas was fifteen feet high and twenty feet long. Famous painters of the old school often painted their scenes from history on canvases that big. But Monet had something different in mind. He wanted to paint twelve people in everyday clothes at a picnic. He had friends come and pose for the picture. It was hard working outdoors on a canvas that big. So, unfortunately, Monet had to break his own rule and take the canvas inside to work on it. He very much hoped to enter this new picture in the Salon, but he couldn't finish it in time.

Instead, he quickly painted a life-size portrait of his

beautiful new girlfriend, Camille. She had white skin and black hair. For the picture she wore a green striped dress and carried a parasol. Again, because of time, he did the painting in his studio. *The Woman in the Green Dress* was accepted for the Salon in 1866 and was a triumph.

Were Monet's father and aunt pleased? No! They were furious. They had found out that Monet and Camille were living together but were not married. Once again his father stopped his allowance.

Claude was twenty- five years old and Camille was nineteen. They had no money—in fact they owed money. They left Paris and rented a house in a small town. Monet started on another big picture—not as big as the picnic painting, but still big. It was eight feet by seven feet and showed four women among trees and flowers. Camille posed for all four women. Monet swore he would paint everything outdoors. He dug a trench in the garden, so he could lower the canvas when he wanted to work on the top part.

Another painter came by one day and asked why he wasn't working on the picture.

"The sun's not shining," Monet said.

His friend suggested that Monet could at least work on the background. But Monet explained that everything—even the background—had to be painted in sunlight. That was the whole point of his art.

The Salon of 1867 turned down his big new picture, *Women in the Garden.* It was too different. The sunlight shining on the dresses and parasols and the shadows from the tree looked strange to the judges.

Monet was almost out of his mind with despair. Nevertheless he kept on painting. He had no money to buy canvases. Sometimes he scraped the paint off old paintings he'd done so he could paint new pictures.

Bazille felt sorry for Monet and bought *Women in the Garden.* He promised to send some of the money every month. But lots of times he forgot. Monet was desperate.

Camille was going to have a baby. Sometimes there wasn't enough money for food.

Monet was in a jam. He took Camille to Paris where he sold two pictures. He gave the money to Camille so that she had something to live on. Then Monet went back alone to Le Havre. He decided to pretend to his parents that he and Camille had broken up.

Back in Le Havre he worked like crazy. Every bit of money he earned would go to Camille. He painted twenty pictures—people, landscapes, seascapes. More than anything, he hoped to afford to be with Camille when the baby came. But on August 8, 1867, little Jean was born without his father there.

Finally Monet's aunt took pity on him and gave him money for train fare to Paris. He and Camille and the baby lived in a small rented room. It was freezing cold that winter, and the family sometimes went without heat or enough food.

Bad luck seemed to follow Monet everywhere. He

sold no paintings. He and Camille and the baby moved to a cheaper place in the country. But when he couldn't pay the rent there either, the landlady threw them out. She kept his clothes, canvases, paints, and brushes.

Now, except for his family, Monet had nothing.

Chapter 3

Bad Times and Good Times

It is hard to imagine things getting any worse for Monet. And fortunately, at last, his luck changed . . . at least a little bit. A rich man in Le Havre wanted paintings—paintings by Monet. He wanted some portraits. So Monet did them as fast as he could. The man also bought two paintings of the sea.

With this money, Monet rented a cottage for his family in a little town on the coast near Le Havre. He kept on working outside, experimenting with light and shadows. He studied the light, so he could make the light in his paintings look real. He began to use different colors of paint instead of black to paint shadows. He stopped mixing colors on his palette. Instead he painted pure colors right on the canvas.

If he wanted green, Monet put a tiny brush stroke of pure blue paint next to a dot of pure yellow. When he looked at the picture, his eyes blended the blue and the yellow and saw green. He once said, "When you go out to paint, try to forget what objects you have before you, a tree, a house, a field, or whatever. Merely think, here is a little square of blue, here an oblong of pink, here a streak of yellow, and paint it just as it looks to you, the exact color and shape."

That summer, Monet spent a lot of time with his old friend, Pierre- Auguste Renoir. The two painters worked outdoors together, side by side. Monet was still poor. Renoir was poor, too. But he was living with his parents. Sometimes he would bring over bread for Monet's family to keep them from starving.

The two friends may have been poor and hungry, but they loved the work they were doing. They both painted pictures of a happy, busy outdoor restaurant on the Seine River. The sun shined on the people and boats and made lovely shadows on the water. Both their paintings of the restaurant would later become famous.

Yet in 1870, once again the Salon rejected Monet's pictures. His best friends—Bazille, Renoir, Sisley, and Pissarro—all had paintings accepted that year.

It was a hard time. But one good thing happened that year. Camille's parents said they would forgive her and even help support little Jean if she and Monet were married. So that's what Claude and Camille did. The wedding was in Paris. None of Monet's family came.

The bride and groom and little Jean went to a beach resort near Le Havre. Boudin and his wife joined them there. Monet painted pictures of Camille on the beach. Over the years, he was to paint her many, many times—on hillsides, in poppy fields, with a parasol, in a garden—often with little Jean at her side.

In July, France went to war with the country of Prussia. (Prussia became part of what today is modern Germany.)

Monet had a family to support; he fled to England to avoid the army.

In London, he painted just as furiously as he had in France. And he had another stroke of luck. An older French painter introduced him to an important art dealer. His name was Paul Durand-Ruel. Durand-Ruel had a gallery in London as well as in Paris. Durand-Ruel saw Monet's talent. He bought several paintings and paid him well.

After the war ended, Monet didn't return to France right away. He took his family to Holland. They settled near Amsterdam where Monet painted canals and windmills and tulips.

In 1871, they went back to France and rented a house in a little town on the Seine River. Monet always liked to be near water. More than anything, he loved to paint water. He turned out nearly fifty pictures the first year.

Finally, Monet was making some real money. His family had enough to eat. Monet bought a barge, which he turned

Japanese Prints

one day monet bought some groceries that were wrapped in paper that turned out to be Japanese prints.

Monet was fascinated with these woodcut prints, as were many other Impressionist painters. They admired the bright colors, flat, two- dimensional style, and compositions that were often off-center.

Over the years Monet collected many prints by noted Japanese artists. They still hang in his house at Giverny. Japanese prints gave him the idea for the Japanese bridge he built over the pond there.

into a floating studio so he could paint in the middle of the river.

France was at peace and times were good. Durand-Ruel came back to Paris and bought more pictures from Monet. Monet painted pictures of the river, the fields, and Camille and Jean outdoors. It was a happy time.

Chapter 4

A New "Salon"

Year after year, Monet' s paintings were still being rejected by the Salon. More often than not, his three friends—Renoir, Pissarro, and Sisley— were also turned down. They all thought their pictures looked fresh and lively, even if critics said they looked "sketchy" and "unfinished."

Monet thought that if they were ever going to make any money, they had to put on their own show.

So in 1874, that's what they did.

It started two weeks before the Salon show opened. Thirty artists took part.

Each day only about one hundred people came to look at their pictures, while thousands flocked to the Salon.

Visitors to the show made fun of it. Not many pictures were sold. People were puzzled by the dabs of bright paint on a canvas. They said each artist must have loaded a gun with paint and fired away at a canvas. They made the most jokes about Monet's paintings. A critic wrote that "Monsieur Monet . . . seems to have declared war on beauty."

One of Monet's paintings was of two little boats with a red sun rising. The picture needed a title for the exhibit catalog. Monet decided to call it *Impression: Sunrise*. What made him choose this name? Monet and his friends often talked about the importance of catching the first impression of a scene in a painting.

People made fun of the title. Soon all the painters in the show were being called "Impressionists." It was meant as an insult. But Monet and the other painters cheerfully agreed that they were indeed Impressionists.

The Impressionists continued to hold their own show for several years. At the one in 1875, police had to keep people from destroying the canvases with canes and umbrellas. Only a few pictures were sold, and those brought very low prices.

Monet once again was asking his friends for loans. Things looked really dark in the fall of 1876, when Camille became ill.

Once again, a rich art collector came to Monet's rescue. This time a man named Ernest and his wife Alice bought lots of Impressionist paintings. They were part owners of a Paris department store and they had a large, beautiful home not far from Paris. Ernest asked Monet to come stay there and paint some panels in one of the rooms.

In 1876, Monet spent all summer working at Ernest's house. Camille and Jean joined him there for part of the time. They had good food, servants, and pleasant company. It must have been a wonderful rest for Camille, who was thin and sick.

Once back in Paris, Monet became interested in painting train stations. He painted the crowds, the steam coming from the huge, black locomotives, and the sky through the glass roof of the station. One stationmaster liked to help out Monet. He would order the engineers to blow white smoke if that was what Monet wanted for a picture.

However, at the next Impressionists' show, visitors hated the train station pictures, too. One man demanded the money for his ticket back. Monet earned very little money from his paintings. He had to give sixteen pictures to an art supplies dealer in order to pay the bill for his paints. Worst of all, Camille was growing sicker. She was also expecting another baby.

Chapter 5

Hardest Times

The Monets' second child, a little boy named Michel, was born in the spring of 1878. Camille's health was worse than ever. Ernest lost all his money so he and his wife Alice and their six children moved in with the Monets. Everyone lived in a big house that had steep steps leading down to the Seine.

Alice did the housekeeping and looked after Camille and the baby Michel. She also gave piano lessons to earn money. Ernest never paid his share of household expenses and ran up bills.

It was a long, hard winter. The cold weather broke records. It started snowing on November 29 and kept on snowing all through December. The snow was several feet deep. Trains often didn't run. Often the roads were blocked. When the Seine froze, the children had fun walking across the river to the town on the other side. The grown-ups, however, were worried and miserable. Monet continued to paint outdoors. Sometimes he would wear three coats and use a hot water bottle to stay as warm as possible.

A neighbor came to their rescue. He bought some of Monet's pictures, which kept everyone from starving.

Monet sent twenty-nine pictures to the Impressionist salon that year. Mary Cassatt, an American painter in Paris, bought one of them for three hundred dollars. But many people still thought his style was odd looking. One art reviewer said he must have done all twenty-nine paintings in one afternoon.

Besides all the money troubles, Camille was dying of cancer. Monet was frantic to find a way to pay for the doctor and Camille's medicine. He pawned everything to raise as much cash as he could.

And for the first time, he could not paint.

Camille, in great pain, died on September 5, 1879.

Strange as it sounds, Monet decided to paint one last picture of her on her deathbed. He was shocked to discover that even in grief, he noticed the way the light shone on the still face of his beloved wife. In the picture, she does not look like an angel at peace. She looks like a dead woman. He was a slave to his art, he admitted to a friend. Nothing mattered more to him.

Alice and her children remained in the house with Monet and his two boys. The next winter was as cold as the one before. The Seine froze solid again. All eight children were sick.

Monet was painting again and worked on many pictures of the Seine that winter. He never grew tired of studying the effect of light on ice and snow. After the thaw came, chunks of ice floated down the river. Monet painted them, too, using gloomy grays and dark purples. When these pictures were put up for sale, everyone said they looked even more unfinished than his usual work.

In a town on the coast near Le Havre, he painted seascapes. One day a heavy rain began to fall. A storm was brewing. Monet decided to try and paint it. He set up his easel on a cliff overlooking the sea and latched it down with rope. He kept painting while waves broke against the cliff just below him. The waves got higher. Monet painted away.

Then a giant wave came in and knocked him off his perch into the water. Monet was almost swept out to sea. He survived by holding on to the rope tied to his easel. Then at last, two fishermen in a boat rescued him.

Soon after this adventure, Monet moved everyone closer to Paris where there was a good school for little Jean. Alice and her six children were now a permanent part of the family. Alice felt that the two Monet boys needed her.

The family did not stay long in the new house. Monet

said he couldn't paint there because the light was all wrong. Nevertheless, he made more money that year, 1882, than he ever had. The end for Monet was when the Seine overflowed and flooded the first floor. It was time to find a proper place with wonderful light where he could settle down and paint.

He searched up and down villages along the Seine River. At last he came upon a house that was nearly perfect for him. It was in a town called Giverny. He stayed there for forty-three years, the rest of his life.

Chapter 6

Giverny

Monet first saw Giverny in April. Apple trees were in bloom and wild flowers sparkled in the fields.

Monet was on a train, but he got off. Right beside the main road was a big farmhouse for rent. It was beautiful. The walls were pink; it had a slate roof and gray shutters. At each end of the house was a low barn with a dirt floor.

The house came with two acres of land that included an apple orchard and a walled garden. A path led down to the railway and, on the other side of the tracks, was a small river.

It was an ideal spot for a painter. Monet could see willow trees and all sorts of plants along the river, and lines of tall poplars marking the edges of meadows. "I can produce masterpieces here," Monet said.

He first rented the house. (Later on he bought it.) The family came with all their furniture and Monet's boats. He now had four—the studio boat, two rowboats, and a skiff. He moored the boats at a place called Nettle Island. It was an easy walk from the house to Nettle Island.

Monet turned one of the dirt-floored barns into a studio. Later, he built a second studio that was much larger and had a skylight. He planted a vegetable garden. It was the job of the children to weed and water it. He tore out the hedges around the gardens. They looked too neat and orderly. He also began work on a big flower garden. (Irises were his favorite flower.) He planted climbing roses on metal arches over the walkways and filled the flower beds with all sorts of plants and flowers. He wanted to make sure there was something blooming from early spring until late fall.

Next to painting, the garden at Giverny became the most important thing in his life. It, too, was a work of art.

Monet was a man of habit. He got up every day at sunrise, ate some bread and sausage, and set out with his palette and paints and easel in a wheelbarrow. He wore a beret and wooden shoes like the local farmers wore. He came back home for lunch. It was always served at 11:30 A.M. on the dot. After the meal, he would drink a cup of coffee in his studio and sometimes a glass of brandy as well. Then he went back to paint outside if the light was still good.

When he was pleased with his work, the whole family was happy. If a picture didn't turn out the way he wanted it to, he got rid of it. Monet had a terrible temper. Once he was painting on his studio boat and got so mad at the way the picture looked that he threw the canvas in the river and his paints and brushes after it. He swore that he would never paint again.

The next day, of course, he had changed his mind. The trouble was that it was Sunday. No art supply store was open. Monet sent a telegram to a paint dealer in Paris. The man opened his store and sent everything Monet needed on the next train to Giverny.

Many things could upset Monet. If a meal was bad or a tree branch fell in the garden, it could send him into a rage.

In spite of bad moments like this, life was so much better than it had ever been. Monet paid more attention to the children—Alice's children, as well as his own sons, Jean and Michel. During school vacations, all eight children and Alice went with Monet to the countryside. While he painted, the children found plenty of ways to enjoy themselves. Blanche painted. Michel fished. Suzanne read. Alice sewed. The younger boys liked to catch frogs. In the summer, they all went swimming from the studio boat, taking turns diving off the roof of the cabin into the water. In the winter, they went ice-skating on the frozen river.

Monet was in his forties, tall and handsome, with a huge beard. Alice was good-looking, smart, and friendly. She understood Monet and admired his work. In 1892, Alice and

Monet were married. And life continued happily.

By this time, public opinion was changing. People were beginning to admire Impressionist paintings. Monet made more money. There was now a cook and an assistant cook at Giverny. One of his favorite dishes was red beans cooked in wine. He also liked goose liver and fancy mushrooms called truffles.

Lots of guests came to visit. Besides having such a large family, Monet kept up with many friends, painters, and writers. He and Alice also liked to spend time in Paris seeing friends. They enjoyed going to a concert, the opera, or a wrestling match.

As for his art, Monet began painting series of pictures. Each series would be of the same object or of the same scene shown in different light.

One of the first of these series were paintings of rows of poplar trees along the river. Monet painted a picture of the poplars early in the morning, then one around noon, and another in late evening. He painted the trees on a cloudy day, in bright sunshine. He painted them in all seasons—in spring, summer, fall, and winter.

One day he heard that some of his favorite poplars were going to be cut down and sold for lumber. Monet paid to have the trees remain for a few months longer so he could finish painting them.

Monet also painted haystacks in the fields. These haystacks were fifteen to twenty feet tall. Just as he had with the poplars, he painted the haystacks again and again in different light at different times of the year. He would arrive in the fields with a wheelbarrow full of canvases. Sometimes one of Alice's daughters would also come along, bringing a second wheelbarrow with more canvases.

Monet would start painting on one canvas. As the day wore on and the light changed, he would put it aside and start another. The next day, he would go back to the first canvas and do more work on it. He'd paint each canvas at the same time every day. It was so important to him that the light remained constant.

Monet worked on another famous series of paintings of a cathedral in the city of Rouen. For these pictures, he rented a small room across from the cathedral and set up his easel by the window. Again, he tried to paint different effects, working when the weather was misty, when there was bright sunshine, and at different times of the day in different seasons. This series of paintings was immensely popular and the cathedral paintings sold for large sums of money. They were shown in exhibits around the world.

Claude Monet was famous now.

His garden was famous, too. Strangers came to Giverny to look at the amazing flowers in the garden. Painters from all over the world came to Giverny, hoping to learn from Monet. (He told them: "Look at nature.") At one time, over forty American painters were renting rooms near Monet's house in Giverny.

The lady who ran a café in town learned to cook things that the American visitors liked, such as baked beans. She even served them a Thanksgiving dinner. Some of the Americans liked Giverny so much that they ended up buying houses there.

Alice and Claude's children were becoming adults. Jean Monet trained as a chemist in Switzerland. Then he went to work for his uncle in Rouen. Jean fell in love and later married Alice's daughter Blanche. Jean and Blanche lived in Rouen. But they came back to Giverny every weekend.

Michel Monet and Alice's son Jean-Pierre were almost the same age. They were stepbrothers, but they also became very close friends. They were both interested in flowers and plants. Jean-Pierre even wrote a book with a family friend about the plants in the area.

Michel and Jean-Pierre were also crazy about bicycles and engines. Jean-Pierre devised a bicycle for two that had a motor. Michel built a gas-powered vehicle that looked like an early automobile.

Michel never had a job. He liked living on the farm at Giverny. And Monet liked having Michel around. The story is that the father and son never talked much. They simply greeted each other in the morning by saying " Bonjour, Monet," and "Au revoir, Monet" when they went to bed.

Chapter 7

The Garden and the Water Lilies

Monet spent more and more time and money on his garden. He enriched the chalky soil. He bought rare plants. He built more trellises for roses. He bought more land for a vegetable garden so he could use all the beds in his garden for flowers. At one point he had six gardeners working for him. But Monet was always in charge.

With so much money coming in, Monet was able to buy some land across from his house. There, the river formed a small pond where arrowheads and water lilies grew. Monet added more water lilies, all different kinds. A few years later he bought more land so he could enlarge his pond. He had to have ditches dug to bring water from the river to fill his pond.

It ended up being three times bigger than the original pond.

In 1892, he began to paint pictures of water lilies. This was his last and probably most famous series. He painted the lilies and their reflections in the water.

Sadly, Alice was now suffering from a blood disease called leukemia. Her doctors could do nothing to save her. She died in 1911.

Monet was desolate without her. He was seventy years old. Often he was dizzy and weak. Worst of all, his eyesight was failing. He had cataracts, which are like thick layers of film that cover the irises. They changed how he saw colors.

Then his son Jean Monet died. Jean was only forty-seven years old. His wife Blanche came back to Giverny and helped to take care of her step-father.

Because of grief and fear for his eyes, Monet did not paint for a while.

When Monet finally picked up a brush again, he began to paint more water lilies. Now he no longer started work as soon as it was light, but waited until his water lilies opened around noon. In 1909, forty-eight water lily pictures were in a show in Paris. People loved the paintings and said they were not like any other pictures in the world.

He began working on huge murals of the water lilies. These paintings were far bigger than any Monet had ever done before. He wanted to see these murals placed permanently in a huge circular room.

In 1918, at the end of World War I, Georges Clemenceau, the prime minister of France came to Giverny. He was a friend of Monet's and asked the artist to give the water lily paintings to France. Monet agreed to donate twelve big panels if they would be displayed in a round room where visitors could stand in the middle and be surrounded by water lilies.

The French government would not build a special building. However, there was an empty building near the Louvre Museum. It was called the Orangerie because it was where orange trees were once grown for the royal family of France. The water lily panels could hang in two oval-shaped rooms on the first floor. The government agreed that nothing else would be exhibited there.

Monet said painting was now the only thing left in his life that gave him any pleasure. Yet because Monet's eyesight was now much worse, he often wasn't satisfied with the work he did. And if he didn't like a painting, he always wanted to get rid of it. He'd cut up canvases, although sometimes Michel and Blanche would save the pieces.

Finally, when he was nearly blind, his family convinced Monet to have surgery on his eye. After two operations and new glasses, he could see well enough to paint. However, afterward he often complained about the way he saw colors.

By 1918 he had finished thirty large canvases, but he refused to sell any of them. He was nearly eighty. Yet every day he set out for the water lily pond. Two gardeners carried his easel and canvases down the path and set everything up for him.

He was very ill now. Monet had been a chainsmoker all his life and he had developed lung cancer. However, right up until the day he died on December 5, 1926, Monet worked on the water lilies. And until the very end, he was still planning new things for his garden. He was excited because some new Japanese water lily bulbs had arrived and he was eager to plant them.

Today people flock to museums to see Monet' s paintings. His large water lily paintings still hang in the Orangerie. The smaller water lily paintings hang in museums all over the world.

Michel Monet was eighty-eight years old when he died. He had no children so he left many beautiful paintings by his father to a museum in Paris. Among them is the one of the boat at sunrise that gave Impressionism its name.

The paintings by the man who often could not keep food on the table now bring prices that would have astonished

Monet. One of the water lily paintings he did in 1904 sold in 2007 for $36.8 million. Monet wanted his work to sell. But money was never the most important thing to him.

When his water lily murals first went on view in the Orangerie museum, a reviewer marveled at the magical portraits of flowers in water and Monet's amazing talent to catch "fleeting moments."

This truly sums up what Monet had been doing all his life—painting fleeting moments in nature.

Giverny Today

After Claude Monet died, his son Michel inherited the house. He did not live there, however. Blanche, Jean's wife, looked after the house and gardens until she died in 1947.

after Michel's death in 1966, several American foundations helped raise money to bring the house and its gardens back to glory. It is now open to the public from April through October. Thousands of visitors come each year.

Timeline of Claude Monet's Life

1840	Claude Monet is born.
1858	Monet meets the painter Eugene Boudin.
1859	Monet moves to Paris and enters the Académie Suisse.
1861	Monet joins the Zouaves.
1862	Monet meets Bazille, Renoir, and Sisley.
1865	Monet meets Camille Doncieux.
1867	Son Jean is born.
1874	Monet exhibits *Impression: Sunrise* at the first Impressionist exhibition.
1878	Son Michel is born.
1879	Camille dies.
1883	Monet moves into the house at Giverny.
1892	Monet marries Alice Hoschedé.
	Monet begins to paint pictures of the water lilies.
1911	Alice dies.
1914	Jean dies.
1926	Monet dies.
1927	Orangerie Museum displays the *Water Lilies* series.

Timeline of the World

1840	The world's first adhesive postage stamp, the Penny Black is used.
1848	The California Gold Rush begins.
1853	Vincent van Gogh is born.
1860	Florence Nightingale founds the first professional school for nurses in England.
1865	The Thirteenth Amendment to the United States Constitution ends slavery in the United States.
1870	The Franco-Prussian war begins.
1876	*The Adventures of Tom Sawyer* by Mark Twain is published.
	Alexander Graham Bell invents the telephone.
1886	The Statue of Liberty is dedicated in New York Harbor.
1888	The first Kodak box camera is sold.
1889	The Eiffel Tower is built in Paris, France.
1898	Marie Curie discovers radium.
1901	Walt Disney is born.
1913	The *New York World* newspaper publishes crossword puzzles for the first time.
1914	World War I begins.
1927	The J*azz Singer* debuts as the first talking film.

Bibliography

Barrier Bjork, Christine. Linnea in Monet's Garden. Farrar, Straus, and Giroux, New York, 1987.

Muhlberger, Richard. What Makes A Monet A Monet? Viking Juvenile, New York, 2002.

Packard, Steven. Smart About Art: Claude Monet: Sunshine and Waterlilies. Grosset & Dunlap, New York, 2001.

Venezia, Mike. Monet. Children's Press, Chicago, 1990.

Waldron, Ann. First Impressions: Claude Monet. Harry N. Abrams, New York, 1991.

Welton, Jude. Eyewitness Books: Monet. DK Publishing, Inc., New York, 1999.

Where to Find Monet Paintings

Now that you know all about Claude Monet's life, you should see his paintings. Many museums in the United States have at least one painting by Monet. Here is a list of larger museums that have many Monet paintings in their permanent collections:

The Museum of Fine Arts – Boston, MA
Art Institute of Chicago – Chicago, IL
The Getty – Los Angeles, CA
Metropolitan Museum of Art – New York, NY
Philadelphia Museum of Art – Philadelphia, PA
National Gallery of Art – Washington, DC

Try to visit one if you can!